The Cunning Plan

Written by
Cath Jones

Illustrated by
Alex Patrick

Shaun's Shop

Way back in time, there was a shopkeeper called Shaun.

He had a big shop and lots of cash.
But he was a mean man!

Dog and Chimp had a little home in a ditch, near Shaun's shop.

Dog was thin and had a limp. Each day she sat and looked with longing at the meat in Shaun's shop.

A few people said, "Shaun, can Dog have a treat?"

But Shaun said, "No! Treats cost me cash. Shoo, Dog!"

Chimp saw how mean Shaun was. She felt sad for Dog.

"We need to teach Shaun a lesson," Chimp said to Dog. "We need to hatch a cunning plan!"

The next time Shaun popped out of his shop,
Dog crept in and snatched a chunk of meat.

But just then, Shaun came back!

Shaun clutched at the meat, but Dog ran off!

Shaun ran out of the shop.
"Come back!" he yelled.
He was going to catch Dog.

This was all part of Dog and Chimp's cunning plan!

Next, Chimp went into the shop and took some things. She took some coins, a silver ring and a bag of cash.

Then Chimp hid up the chimney.

When Shaun came back, he spotted the thefts! Then Chimp popped out from the chimney.

Shaun looked at Chimp, then tried to snatch her.

"Wait!" said Chimp. "I can get back the missing things. Let's make a pact."

"What sort of pact?" Shaun asked.

"If you beat Dog in a running match, you will get back the missing things. But if Dog wins, she gets free food from you each day, from now on."

"I agree!" said Shaun.

Lots of people came to see the contest.

When Chimp shouted "Go!", Shaun ran like a shot. He was quick.

Dog limped. She was not so quick.

"Now for the plan!" said Chimp.

First, she threw the coins onto the ground. Shaun stopped and picked up all the coins, one at a time.

Meanwhile, Dog kept going!

Shaun ran to catch up with Dog.

Next, Chimp hung the silver ring in a tree. Shaun stopped. He found a stick and fished the ring out of the tree.

Meanwhile, Dog kept going!

Now, Chimp tipped up the bag of cash.

Shaun stopped to pick it all up.

Meanwhile, Dog kept going!
And look! Now the finish line is near!

Shaun ran, but he was too far back to catch up. Dog was the winner!

Shaun's greed lost him the contest, but he did get his things back.

And now, each day, Dog goes to get free treats from Shaun.